YOUR KNOWLEDGE HAS VALUE

Wiebke Marie von Bremen

Aus der Reihe: e-fellows.net stipendiaten-wissen

e-fellows.net (Hrsg.)

Band 1486

Does denying same sex-marriage conflict with the American Dream?

GRIN Publishing

Bibliographic information published by the German National Library:

The German National Library lists this publication in the National Bibliography; detailed bibliographic data are available on the Internet at http://dnb.dnb.de .

Imprint:

Copyright © 2012 GRIN Verlag, Open Publishing GmbH
Print and binding: Books on Demand GmbH, Norderstedt Germany
ISBN: 978-3-668-00619-5

This book at GRIN:

http://www.grin.com/en/e-book/302228/does-denying-same-sex-marriage-conflict-with-the-american-dream

GRIN - Your knowledge has value

Since its foundation in 1998, GRIN has specialized in publishing academic texts by students, college teachers and other academics as e-book and printed book. The website www.grin.com is an ideal platform for presenting term papers, final papers, scientific essays, dissertations and specialist books.

Visit us on the internet:

http://www.grin.com/

http://www.facebook.com/grincom

http://www.twitter.com/grin_com

Josef-Albers-Gymnasium in Bottrop
Städtisches Gymnasium für Jungen und Mädchen
-Sekundarstufen I und II-

Does denying same-sex marriage conflict with the American Dream?
Facharbeit im Leistungskurs Englisch (E1*)

Vorgelegt von: Wiebke Marie von Bremen

Jahrgangsstufe: 12

Schuljahr: 2011/12

Abgabetermin: 20.04.2012

Table of Contens

1. Introduction

The dream of an America with boundless possibilities has shaped the American society over centuries. As the historian James Truslow Adams defined the phrase "The American Dream" in 1931, it is the "dream of a land, in that life should be better and richer and fuller for everyone, with the opportunity for each according to ability or achievement" and in that everyone should "be recognized by others for what they are, regardless of the furtuitous circumstances of birth or position"[1]. The idea of the American dream is rooted in the United States´ Declaration of Independence which declares that "all men are created equal, that they are endowed by their Creator with certain inalienable rights, that among these are Life, Liberty and the Pursuit of Happiness"[2].

However there are issues like homosexuality and same-sex marriage that, with regard to the ban on same-sex marriage present in most of the United States, seem to be contrary to the notion of the American Dream. Thus one has to ask: Don´t gays/lesbians deserve the Pursuit of Happiness and the same rights as heterosexuals? Does marriage fit in as an inalienable right? Or quite simply, does denying same-sex marriage conflict with the American Dream?

In the following I am going to deal with those questions under close examination of the present situation in the United States, same-sex marriage beeing the new civil rights dispute and in that context the supporting and opposing arguments, as well as the California ballot Propositon 8 and the situation of children of gay parents. Further I am going to include the results of an interview with a lesbian couple that lives in North California with its 7 year old daughter.

---

[1] Truslow Adams, J.: The Epic of America. New York 1938, p. 412
[2] Adams, J.; Jefferson, T.; Fanklin, B.; a. o.: The Declaration of Independence, 1776

2. Present Situation

At present there are approximately 1.2 Million gay couples living in the United States, so the total number of gay couples amounts to about 594,391. Thereof, with a quantity of 92,138, California is the state with the most gay couples. Altogether gay people make up 1-4% of the population in all cities and especially concentrate in metropolian areas like Washington D.C. that registers the highest concentration of gay couples (1.29%).[3]

Yet gay marriage is merely legal in 6 U.S. states –Massachusetts, Connecticut, Iowa, Vermont, New Hampshire, New York- and Washington D.C.. New York solely recognizes out-of-state gay marriages and so does California, however only if the marriage is from before Proposition 8 was passed. New Jersey recognizes civil unions between same-sex couples and several states have domestic partnership laws that grant certain benefits to them.[4] "On the flip side, thirty states have passed constitutional amendments or laws explicitly banning same-sex marriage".[5]

But on the social level, the general visibility and acceptance of homosexuality has increased, especially during the past few years and especially among younger generations. This is last but not least a consequence of LGBT (lesbian, gay, bisexual, and transgender) social movements and a soaring awareness due to globalization. As it becomes more and more acceptable for homosexuals to acknowledge their sexual orientations in public, more and more commit themselves to their partners for life. Hence, as the call for legal gay marriage or equal access to civil marriage for same-sex couples becomes more visible and the issue more public, the imperative to solve the issue also increases.

---

[3] data taken from: Alper,G.: The Gay Law Report. Insight& Analysis of LGBT Legal Issue and related News. Gay Marriage Facts& Statistics. Nov 1, 2010. Released: http://www.gaylawreport.com/gay-marriage-facts-statistics/. Last update: March 27, 2012

[4] data taken from: Alper,G.: The Gay Law Report

[5] Jones, M.: A Few Statistics on LGBT ISSUE. Change.org. Oct 5, 2008. Released: http://news.change.org/stories/a-few-statistics-on-lgbt-issues. Last update: March 27, 2012

3. The New Civil Rights Dispute

The United States is quite obviously one of the most diverse nations of the world. It is home to people of various races, religions and cultures with various traditions, beliefs and values. While this diversity provides special and irreplacable contribution to the country, it also pulls the trigger for a great number of disputes, civil rights issues beeing the most intense of them.

We have seen the colonist successfully fight for their independence and founding the United States of America. We have seen women, campaign for and finally beeing granted the right to vote. And we have seen the long, brutal struggle of African-Americans eking out their way from slavery, over segregation and racism to eventual freedom and equality. All those people fought for what they believed in and dreamed of, for what they found to be their inalienable right and for what they needed to achieve their own personal Pursuit of Happiness, with social acceptance always coming before the legal.

The new, present civil rights dispute centers around homosexuality and, while beeing more and more accepted on the social level, the access for gay people to legal marriage. The debate confronts a great range of opposing and favoring arguments, that rest upon religion, tradition, history, ethics, politics, and last but not least the quintessence of the American Dream.

3.1. Opposition: Biblical and Natural Law Arguments

The most common oppositional view towards homosexuality is fairly simple. It states that homosexuality is an aberration that requires a cure, so it declares all human beeings as beeing essentially heterosexual. For the sake of simplicity, lets call this view the prohibitionist view.

Many of the prohibitionist arguments are based on religious grounds. The Bible, or more precisely the Old Testament professes homosexuality as a breach of the covenant with God. For instance, in Levitikus 18:22 it says very clearly:" Though shalt not lie with mankind as with womankind; it is an abomination (...) If a man also lie with mankind, as he lieth with a woman, both of them have commited an abomination; they shall surely be put to death; their blood shall be upon them." In Romans 1:26-27 Saint Paul writes: "For this cause God gave them up into vile affections: for even their women did change the natural use into that which is against nature: And likewise also the men, leaving the natural use of the woman, burned in their lust one toward another; men with men working that which is unseemly, and receiving in themselves that recompense of their error which was meet." So as beeing gay in general is defined as beeing an anathema to God, gay marriage in particular is not even considered in the Scripture.

The modern, prohibitionist view on homosexuality is not primarily scripturally based, but rests upon the theory of natural law. Natural law theory originated in Genesis and was elaborated by Aristotle. The most influential interpretation of natural law theory, however, descends from Thomas Aquinas, a philosopher, theologian and Dominican friar living in medieval Italy. He "took the notion of an individuals nature and universalized it. Drawing on Aristotle´s conception of normative nature, Aquinas theorized that all human beeings had a single fundamental nature and a single natural end."[6] And as the natural end of the sex act is to procreate, all human beeings` sexuality is linked to procreation. On the contrary, in this view, "homosexuality is against the order of the universe"[7], so against natural law. Pushed by the Roman Catholic Church, this view spread all across Western civilization. On this basis prohibitionists argue that only heterosexual marriage, given the possibility of marital procreation, is a divinely ordained bond.

Furthermore, opponents of homosexuality see a threat of social and familial stability in the issue of same-sex marriage. They fear that its acknowledgement would undermine the traditional family live which, with regard to the anyway "unprecedent state of collapse"[8] of families nowadays, was urgently to be prevented if we wanted to preserve the human race.

---

[6] Sullivan,A.: Virtually Normal: An Argument About Homosexuality. New York, 1995. Position 447
[7] Sullivan,A.: Position 459
[8] Sullivan, A.: Position 1441

3.2. Support: Liberal and Constitutional Arguments

Yet the prohibitionist´s argumentations are countered by an increasingly-acknowledged view in favor of gay marriage that, in my oppinion, easily outdoes the opposition.

Regarding the befliefs which rely upon religious grounds, supporters claim that refusing to accept homosexuality is a refusal to acccept the complexity of God´s creation, a refusal to accept "the human person, made in the image and likeness of God."[9] This certainly is a matter of belief; however, religious arguments are quite simply condemned by the fact of the United States being a liberal democracy. "One of the first principles of liberal societies, as they have emerged from theocracies and dictatorships of the past, is that the religious is not the same as the political"[10], meaning that church and state are seperated. Many of the first European settlers who came to the former Colonial America a couple of centuries ago dreamed of finding religious freedom, as they were beeing persecuted for their faith at home. The Constitution of the United States now forbids the constraint of people into unwilling obedience to religious authority. The American Dream is rooted on human freedom and equality.

As for the natural law arguments and the position that only marriage between a man and a women meets its procreative purpose, supporters answer: "Marriages are available to sterile or older couples without the possibility of having children"[11] and gay couples in fact are finding ways to have and raise children.

Furthermore the 14th Amendment (adopted in 1868) of the Constitution that deals with the civil rights of the citizen, plays an important role regarding equality for homosexuals. Its Equal Protection Clause requires that "no State (...) shall deny to any person within its jurisdiction the equal protections of the laws."[12] Whereas back in 1868 this Amendment was primarily passed to grant equal citizenship to blacks and did not include any language specifically about sexual preferences, supporters demand

---

[9] Cardinal Joseph Ratzinger: Letter of the Pastoral Care of Homosexual Persons, 1986
[10] Sullivan, A.: Position 348
[11] Sullivan, A.: Position 618
[12] United States Constitution, 14th Amendment, Section 1, adopted on July 9, 1868

that due to process it should apply to LGBT people as well. In other words they argue that denying gay people certain rights, in this case the right of marriage, was unconstitiutional.

3.3. Proposition 8

California, with the nation´s largest and most racially diverse gay and lesbian population, has palyed a prominent role in the modern gay marriage debate, regarding the contested ruling of Prop 8.

Prop 8, officially titled "Proposition 8- Eliminates Right of Same-Sex Couples to Marry", was a ballot proposition in California passed in the November 2008 state elections. It limited marriage to only one man and one woman by adding the amendment "only marriage between a man and a woman is valid or recognized in California"[13] to the Califorina Constitution. It was passed by California voters by a margin of 52 percent to 48 percent.

Since its adoption, Prop 8 has been the issue of court actions and has continued to be one of the central battlegrounds in the fight over same-sex marriage in the United States. Proponents called it the "Marriage Protection Act" and saw in it the preservation of traditional marriage and parenting. Opponents, however, protested and set a number of legal battles against the, as they sensed it, indefensible, irrational and unconstitutional measure in motion.

The case got to federal court, where Judge Vaughn Walker ruled in August 2010 that "Proposition 8 both unconstitutionally burdens the exercise of the fundamental right to marry and creates an irrational classification on the basis of sexual orientation."[14]

On Feburary 7, 2012, in a 2-1 decision, a three judge panel of the 9th U.S. Circuit Court of Appeals overturned Proposition 8 that was found to be a violation of the Fourteenth Amendment. "Proposition 8 serves no purpose, and has no effect, other than to lessen the status and human dignity of

---

[13] California Constitution, Section 7.5 of the Declaration of Rights, adopted in 2008

[14] Williams, P.: Court: Calif. ban on gay marriage is unconstitutional. NBC news. San Francisco, 2012. Released: http://usnews.msnbc.msn.com/ news/2012/02/07/10342899-court-calif-ban-on-gay-marriage-is-unconstitutional. Last update: April 16, 2012

gays and lesbians in California, and to officially reclassify their relationships and families as inferior", said the liberal Circuit Judge Stephen Reinhardt. "The constitution simply does not allow for this sort of law."[15] However, the court did not primarily focus on the question wether or not the constitution protects the rights of all gay couples to marry, but on the fact that 5 month before Prop 8 passed, the Supreme Court had just legalized same-sex marriage. So gays in California actually held the legal right to marry for a short time, till it was taken away from them again by the passage of Prop 8.

The sponsor group ProtectMarriage now, somewhat ironically, wants the Supreme Court to rule on the case anew and has vowed that they will take on their fight in favor of Proposition 8.

4. Children of Homosexual Parents

Besides their struggle for equal marriage rights and despite the prohibitionists´ argument that gay marriage was not procreative, same-sex couples also fight for their right to have children. And gay men and women in fact are finding ways, be it adoption, co-parrenting arangements, donor inseminations or surrogacy, to have and raise children.

Now common concern is that children of gay parents will grow up to be homosexual or at least confused about their gender themselves, be stigmatized, are more likely to be bullied, will do worse in academics and have less friends than children of heterosexual parents. In other words, many people believe that in general, children of gay parents thrive worse than they would in a hetersosexual houshold. Yet, broad research has shown that, at large, "kids in both heterosexual and homosexual housholds have similar levels of academic achievements, number of friends and overall well-being"[16]. Also there has been no proof that homosexual parenting would seed any kind of gender confusion. So really not gender

---

[15] Dillon, N.: Court rules Prop 8 is unconstitutional. NYDailyNews.com. Februrary 7, 2012. Released: http://articles.nydailynews.com/2012-02-07/news/31035794_1_gay-marriage-marriage-ban-court-rules-prop. Last update: April 16, 2012

[16] Bryner, J.: Childrens Raised by Lesbians Do Just Fine, Studies Show. LiveScience. Feburary 8, 2010. Released: http://www.livescience.com/6073-children-raised-lesbians-fine-studies-show.html. Last update: April 18, 2012

seems to determine good parenting, but in fact the relationship a parent, regardless if male or female, has with his child.

Yet, a concern that certainly can have negative impact on children of gay parents is, again, the concern of gay marriage. As at that time 10 year old Kasey Nicholson-McFadden stated in 2010 in front of the New Jersey State House: "It doesn´t bother me to tell kids my parents are gay. It does bother me to say that they aren´t married. It makes me feel that our family is less than their family."[17] Therefore one can not argue marriage should be denied to same-sex couples as it does not meet its procreative purpose, since that has been proven to be wrong. However, one certainly can argue that marriage should be available especially to same-sex couples with children, to ensure that their parents "lack of marriage benefits"[18] does not have any negative impact on those children.

5. Example: The Life of a Californian Lesbian Couple[19]

I spent my Junior Year of High School as an exchange student in North California, where I meet a lot of openly homosexual people, among them, a lesbian couple that became close friends of mine.

Stephanie S. and Julia C. have been a couple since 1995. By that time Stephanie had already come out about being gay and her family turned out to be very supportive of their relationship. And, as Stephanie says with a smile, "once they met me, her family had an easier time accepting her (Julia's) sexuality"[20] as well.

They are not married, but registered as so called "domestic partners" which is essentially the same as marriage except for the name. Domestic partners possess nearly all the legal rights of married partners, except for they are not entitled to any Federal spousal rights, since they are not federally recognized. While considered married in California, that status is not conceded to them nationwide.

---

[17] Wildman, S.: Children Speak for Same-Sex Marriage. New York Times. January 20, 2010. Released: http://www.nytimes.com/2010/01/21/fashion/21kids.html?_r=3&pagewanted=all. Last update: April 18, 2012
[18] Wildman, S.: Children Speak for Same-Sex Marriage
[19] All names have been anonymized.
[20] Interview, cf. attachments

Stephanie and Julia believe that same-sex marriage should be legalized because "it's a basic human right, quite simply. We have decided that we would get married if it became federally recognized, not state-by-state." [21]

As for the opposing side they answer that they do not see any value in biblical based arguments. Since we would not follow the rules of the Bible as a whole, considering it prohibits piercings for instance, it would not be legitimate to take just some parts literally. Furthermore they do not give credit to procreative arguments either, as there were many married couples without children, in contrast to themselves who actually have a child.

Their daughter Georgia is 7 years old and in her second year of elementary school. Stephanie who always wanted to have children actually is her biological mother. Her dad is an unknown Chinese sperm donor because they wanted their child at least somewhat to look like Julia, who is Chinese, too. According to her parents, Georgia "is totally well-adjusted" and they believe that growing up in a homosexual family "will make her more accepting and open-minded. So far, at 7, she loves being different- says it makes her special!"[22]

---

[21] Interview, cf. attachments
[22] Interview, cf. attachments

5. Conclusion

Coming to a final conclusion, I speak out in favor of gay marriage. I believe that any two adults who love each other, regardless of their sexual orientation, should be accredited with the right to commit themselves to one another for life. Further I deem it as a liberal state´s supreme duty to live up to its promise of equal protection of all citizen under the law.

And to get back to the initial questions:

> ➤ Yes, I do believe that gays and lesbians deserve the Pursuit of Happiness and the same rights as heterosexuals, so anybody for whom marriage and a family are the Pursuit of Happiness deserves to get married.

> ➤ Yes, I do believe that marriage fits in as an inalienable right because I do believe, like the Declaration of Independence states, that "all men are created equal".Therefore, it is every person right to be treated equal, as well.

> ➤ And finally, yes, I do believe that denying same-sex marriage conflicts with the American Dream. Such a denial stands in clear contrast to the dream of an America that is characterized by boundless opportunities, independence, freedom, equality and happiness.

A general legalization of same-sex marriage would not do harm to anybody and it would not legislate private tolerance of homosexuality. However, it would declare public equality and grant gays and lesbians access to a human right that is due to them: To say "Yes, I do." This might seem like a big step forward, but it is the only right one to make. We just need the courage to take action.

6. Bibliography

Print sources:

California Constitution. Section 7.5 of the Declaration of Rights. Adopted in 2008

Jefferson, Thomas; Adams, John; Franklin, Benjamin; a. o.: The Declaration of Independence. Adopted on July 4, 1776

King James Bible, first published in 1611

Ratzinger, Cardinal Joseph: Letter to Bishops of the Catholic Church on the Pastoral Care of Homosexual Persons. In: Harvey, John F., O.S.F.S.: The Homosexual Person. New Thinking in Pastoral Care. Ignatius Press, San Francisco, 1987, p. 235

Sullivan, Andrew: Virtually Normal. An Argument About Homosexuality. Alfred A. Knopf, Inc., New York, 1995. Kindle Edition

Truslow Adams, James: The Epic of America. Routledge, New York 1938[3]

United States Constitution. 14th Amendment, Section 1. Adopted on July 9, 1868

Online sources:

Alper, Jon: The Gay Law Report. Insight& Analysis of LGBT Legal Issue and related News.Gay Marriage Facts& Statistics. Nov 1, 2010. Released: http://www.gaylawreport.com/gay-marriage-facts-statistics/. Last update: March 27, 2012

Balllotpedia: California Proposition 8, the "Eliminates Right of Same-Sex Couples to Marry" Initiative (2008). Released:

http://ballotpedia.org/wiki/index.php/California_Proposition_8,_the_%22Eli
minates_Right_of_Same-
Sex_Couples_to_Marry%22_Initiative_%282008%29. Last update: April
18, 2012

Bryner, Jeanna: Childrens Raised by Lesbians Do Just Fine, Studies
Show. LiveScience. Feburary 8, 2010. Released:
http://www.livescience.com/6073-children-raised-lesbians-fine-studies-
show.html. Last update: April 18, 2012

Dillon, Nancy: Court rules Prop 8 is unconstitutional. NYDailyNews.com.
Februrary 7, 2012. Released: http://articles.nydailynews.com/2012-02-
07/news/31035794_1_gay-marriage-marriage-ban-court-rules-prop. Last
update: April 16, 2012

Jones, Michael: A Few Statistics on LGBT ISSUE. Change.org. Oct 5,
2008. Released: http://news.change.org/stories/a-few-statistics-on-lgbt-
issues. Last update: March 27, 2012

Wildman, Sarah: Children Speak for Same-Sex Marriage. New York
Times. January 20, 2010. Released:
http://www.nytimes.com/2010/01/21/fashion/21kids.html?_r=3&pagewante
d=all. Last update: April 18, 2012

Williams, Pete: Court: Calif. ban on gay marriage is unconstitutional. NBC
news. San Francisco,2012. Released:
http://usnews.msnbc.msn.com/_news/2012/02/07/10342899-court-calif-
ban-on-gay-marriage-is-unconstitutional. Last update: April 16, 2012

7. Attachments

Interview

How long have you two been a couple?

„Since 1995! 17 years this June."

How did and do other people (family, friends, neighbors, ...) respond to you beeing in a relationship?

„By then all of my family knew already that I was gay and were very supportive. My grandmother LOVED Joanne and remembered her more than me as she was dying and suffering from dementia.
Joanne's mom and sister had an easier time accepting her sexuality once they met me."(smiles)

You are not married, but in a domestic partnership. Can you define domestic partnership?

„It's basically the same as marriage except for the name. Our legal status is treated much like marriage, which means we have the responsibilities of a married couple. However, because we are not federally recongnized, we don't have the benefits (automatic hospital visitation, etc.) in all states. We may be forced to show our DP certificate if we travel to another state that doesn't recognize our partnership. We're considered married in CA, but not nation-wide."

Do you think same-sex marriage should be legalized ? And why? And would you like to actually get married?

„Yes. It's a basic human right, quite simply. We have decided that we would get married if it became FEDERALLY recognized, not state-by-state."

How would legally being married change your life?

„Honestly, it wouldn't! We are essentially married—had a ceremony, have a child together, own a home (and a puppy now!), etc. But it would feel good to be part of history."

What is your oppinion on anti-gay marriage arguments like it´s against the Bible, it does not meet ist procreative purpose and it is a threat to stable family life?

„You can't take some parts of the Bible literally and not others...the Bible also states that you shouldn't pierce your ears, get a tatoo, or even mix cotton with polyester. We don't follow that! Plus, many married couples DON'T procreate, and we did, so..."

Since you are California citizen: Did Proposition 8 have any impact on your life?

„Only emotionally. It was disappointing and depressing."

How and when did you decide to have a child?

„I've always wanted one. Kept begging until Joanne said yes." (smiles)

Was it a complicated step to take?

„Not really. It was more medical/scientific...certinaly not romantic or sexual. It was expensive too."

Do you think having gay parents impacts your child?

„She's totally well-adjusted. I'm sure she'll have some issues later in life— but what child doesn't? I think it will make her more accepting and open-

minded. So far, at 7, she LOVES being different—says it makes her special."

How would you answer to the „guideline-questions" of my project?:
Don´t gays/lesbians deserve the Pursuit of Happiness and the same rights as heterosexuals? Does marriage fit in as an inalienable right? Or quite simply, does denying same-sex marriage conflict with the American Dream?

"Yes, yes, yes!"